SUMMARY & ANALYSIS

OF

THIS IS MARKETING

You Can't Be Seen Until You Learn to See

A GUIDE TO THE BOOK
BY SETH GODIN

BY *ZIP*READS

NOTE: This book is a summary and analysis and is meant as a companion to, not a replacement for, the original book.

Please follow this link to purchase a copy of the original book: https://amzn.to/2MiiGc6

TABLE OF CONTENTS

SYNOPSIS

In his book *This is Marketing: You Can't Be Seen Until You Learn to See,* Seth Godin unveils his modern approach to marketing, one that leaves behind the egocentric advertising of the past and grounds itself in empathy. He encourages readers to seek positive change—change that truly matters—through meaningful connections and emotional labor.

Godin's method is based on a simple, yet fundamental principle: marketers exist to serve others. Rather than starting with a product or service and then trying to spread the word and make people care about it, Godin instead advocates the idea that marketing should actively find and solve people's problems.

Using varied and interesting case studies, Godin gives insight into how marketers should abandon the historical tendency to cater to the selfish interests of companies and stop manipulating people by stealing their time and attention, particularly because these techniques are no longer effective in the age of the internet. Instead, he encourages marketers to build on existing narratives, which then form the foundation of powerful and effective marketing.

This is Marketing is a call to action, providing inspiration to make change that you can be proud of, both as a marketer and as a human being.

CHAPTER SUMMARIES & KEY TAKEAWAYS

CHAPTER 1: NOT MASS, NOT SPAM, NOT SHAMEFUL...

In this chapter, Godin begins with a comparison of the outdated and selfish form of marketing that dominated in the past versus marketing today, which depends on having empathy for and serving your customers.

Key Takeaway: Marketing is a generous act.

Marketing today is positive. Godin believes that marketing should build people up, rather than tear them down and prey on their insecurities. Marketing should be about helping people solve real problems and, ultimately, make their lives better. Marketing helps people become who they want to be.

Key Takeaway: The internet was not invented for marketing.

Historically, mass media has served marketers. Television and radio were both invented with advertisers in mind. However, the internet is inherently self-centered, catering to the interests and desires of billions of individuals instead of marketers.

Key Takeaway: Today, marketing is not synonymous with advertising.

It is no longer enough to advertise. You have to reach out and connect with people on a deeper level—churning out advertisements is no longer synonymous with marketing. Getting the word out by trading ads for money won't work. You have to get discovered. Becoming a marketer is about creating ideas that will spread. You should be missed when people notice you are gone and offer more than customers expect.

CHAPTER 2: THE MARKETER LEARNS TO SEE

Godin begins this chapter with a personal anecdote about his own trial-and-error discovery of what makes effective marketing. He then uses the chapter to outline an approach to marketing that he describes as simple, yet difficult to embrace. This approach to marketing is about culture and the human condition.

Key Takeaway: Marketing is about patience, empathy, and respect.

In order to market effectively, you must learn how "to see how human beings dream, decide, and act. And if you help them become better versions of themselves, the ones they seek to be, you're a marketer" (Godin, loc. 262). So marketing is about human connection, which makes it complicated but also extremely rewarding and constructive when done correctly.

Key Takeaway: Marketing can be broken down into five steps.

First, you have to invent something with value. Second, it should benefit a small group of people in a particular way. Third, you must tell a story that meshes with the internal narrative of that group of people. Fourth, spread the word. Fifth and finally, build confidence over time by being present and leading people towards positive change.

Key Takeaway: Marketing is about solving other people's problems.

Marketing does not serve to solve problems for the company. It should solve a problem for the consumer. People don't care about what you care about. To market properly, you must have the empathy to recognize this important fact.

Key Takeaway: Culture is strategy.

When it comes to marketing, approach is key. In order to make change, you must begin by getting people in sync and fostering a common culture. Remember that only committed and creative individuals will manage to change the world.

CHAPTER 3: MARKETING CHANGES PEOPLE

In this chapter, Godin breaks down the concept of stories—the narratives through which people perceive their worlds. Each of us has a unique narrative, and you need to be able to imagine the stories that the people you serve need to hear in order to help them move closer to their dreams and goals.

Key Takeaway: Marketing is about understanding irrational human drives.

"People don't want what you make. They want what it will do for them. They want the way it will make them feel" (Godin, loc. 374).

Marketers are actually selling emotions, not products.

Key Takeaway: A marketer has three tools—stories, connections, and experiences.

Humans naturally feel lonely and seek connection. Every experience that we have builds connection and adds depth to our stories. Being *market*-driven lasts because you are focused on people's hopes, dreams, and frustrations. You seek to create real cultural change rather than manipulating people with *marketing*-driven techniques.

CHAPTER 4: THE SMALLEST VIABLE MARKET

As Godin points out in this chapter, it is boring to fall somewhere in the middle. When it comes to marketing, this is a dead end. Trying to satisfy everyone leads to generalizations and stagnation. Instead of languishing somewhere in the middle, develop a unique and useful product by starting with a simple and targeted group, called your *smallest viable market.*

Minimal entrepreneurship means starting with the simplest version of your product. You then test it by engaging with market and getting feedback. Once you have achieved success with your smallest viable market, you can improve your product, expand your market, and repeat the process.

Key Takeaway: You can't change everyone.

People are too diverse and too indifferent for you (or anyone for that matter) to stand a chance at changing everyone.

Key Takeaway: You can begin to define your market by focusing on their *worldview*.

Rather than focusing on demographics, you should define your smallest viable market based on "psychographics." Different groups tend to tell themselves different stories. This shapes their worldviews—the lens through which they see the world, including their biases and stereotypes.

Key Takeaway: Rejection is inevitable.

Remember, your product is not for everyone. Therefore, you will get harsh feedback, and you will be rejected. You must resist and be secure in the fact that your product is not for them. You do not need to change their minds. This is respectful of their time and beliefs. *"It's impossible to create work that both matters and pleases everyone"* (Godin, loc. 572).

CHAPTER 5: IN SEARCH OF "BETTER"

In this chapter, Godin bases his arguments about "better" on the concept of "sonder," which is defined as *"that moment when you realize that everyone around you has an internal life as rich and conflicted as yours"* (Godin, loc. 617). Because everyone else is just as complicated as you are, you must have empathy in order to understand that "better" is always relative.

Key Takeaway: As a marketer, you will be torn between two extremes.

You have two jobs as a marketer. First, you must be able to create interesting new things for people who get bored easily. These are the individuals who will discover your work first and who will spread the word. Secondly, you also need to build durable products and services that expand beyond that initial group.

Key Takeaway: Be the obvious choice.

Rather than crowding an area where the consumer is already spoiled for choice, create your own niche by combining two concepts that have yet to be combined in that particular way. People are waiting for your product, but they don't know it yet. When people find out about what you have created, it should make them excited and be a clear and easy choice.

CHAPTER 6: BEYOND COMMODITIES

Godin begins this chapter with a reminder that effective marketing does not start with a product. It starts with a group that needs to be served, a determination of their problems, and then, the development of a product that makes a change they are seeking.

Key Takeaway: Quality is no longer enough.

Nowadays, quality is expected. Meeting specifications isn't optional, and your customers know more about your competition than you ever will. Therefore, it's not sufficient to simply do what you say you will do. You have to organize an experience that suits the story your customers are telling themselves. And once you make this promise, you are on the hook to deliver.

Key Takeaway: Authenticity is not the goal.

There is a difference between "presenting" and "revealing." You must remember that your work is to serve. This involves emotional labor—doing things we don't necessarily feel like doing in the moment. As a professional, you are not striving to be constantly authentic. The goal is to present a professional service, to be empathetic, and to serve your client.

CHAPTER 7: THE CANVAS OF DREAMS AND DESIRES

In this chapter, Godin focuses on the universal "needs" and emotions underlying marketing. As he writes,

"The heart and soul of a thriving enterprise is the irrational pursuit of becoming irresistible" (Godin, loc. 1191).

This irresistibility comes from tapping into, understanding, and then fulfilling people's dreams and desires.

Key Takeaway: People don't know what they need.

People tend to think that they "need" things that are actually wants, not needs. Because of privilege, wants are perceived as being needs. And although people are aware of what they want, people are very bad at finding new ways to meet those "needs."

Key Takeaway: Innovative marketing finds new solutions to deal with classic emotions.

After presenting a short list of universal dreams and desires, the author states, "*You could probably add ten more. But it's unlikely you could add fifty more. This core basket of dreams and desires means that marketers, like artists, don't need many colors to paint an original masterpiece*" (Godin, loc. 1098). You are looking for a new solution that will help people to satisfy their dreams and desires in a new way.

CHAPTER 8: MORE OF THE WHO

This chapter builds on chapter four, further defining the idea of the smallest viable market. Godin points out that some customers aren't worth the trouble. You are looking for good customers who will spread the word and get you more customers. This works especially well when sharing is part of your product design. If your product works better when everyone is using it, and growth creates value, people will naturally want to share it with others.

Key Takeaway: Even hits are only meaningful to a few people.

The reason that the smallest viable market works is that you only need a strong core of passionate customers to have a successful product or service.

Key Takeaway: People are right *not* to choose your product.

It is important to remember that people who don't choose your product are right: your product is not for them. You need to be able to recognize and respect why they don't choose your product or service. By recognizing they are right, you win the freedom to stop trying to please everyone and focus on work that matters to your smallest viable audience.

CHAPTER 9: PEOPLE LIKE US DO THINGS LIKE THIS

In this chapter, Godin expands on the idea that individuals act in accordance with their internal narratives. People are driven to fit in and by their perception of status. These two reasons are why marketers often overestimate their ability to make change. You have to understand people's internal narratives in order to make change.

Key Takeaway: Marketing is about normalizing new behavior.

It's cyclical: "Normalization creates culture, and culture drives our choices, which leads to more normalization" (Godin, loc. 1388). You need to begin by defining an "us." This is not culture in general (which is indefinable), but a culture. The goal is to normalize behavior to the extent the group thinks, "people like us act in this way." At the same time, be thoughtful with your innovation. You want to go just a bit farther than what people are already doing. Don't go too far or people won't follow you. Change has to be gradual.

Key Takeaway: Elite and exclusive usually don't coexist.

There is an important difference between being an elite group and being an exclusive one: elite is an external measure, while exclusive is an internal measure. Elite status cannot be controlled or guaranteed. Exclusive groups are the ones who can change a culture because they work as long as the members believe in the change being made and wish to fit in with the other members (the "us").

CHAPTER 10: TRUST AND TENSION CREATE FORWARD MOTION

Godin explains in this chapter that you are doing one of two things as a marketer: "pattern match" or "pattern interrupt." Pattern match fits the story we tell ourselves, while pattern interrupt breaks with the status quo. Therefore, pattern interrupt requires a jolt of energy. This can come when we have to form new patterns due to new life events (marriage, a new baby, etc.) or it can come from a creation of tension.

Key Takeaway: Tension can modify patterns.

In order to achieve a pattern interrupt, a marketer can work to create tension. We don't want to feel left out or uninformed. This tension can be enough to build the momentum needed for change. However, tension is not the same as fear. Fear paralyzes us, and tension is about positive forward momentum.

"All effective education creates tension, because just before you learn something, you're aware you don't know it (yet)" (Godin, loc. 1543).

Key Takeaway: Truth isn't enough.

Truth won't change the status quo. Being right isn't enough. Only cultural change can shift the status quo.

CHAPTER 11: STATUS, DOMINANCE, AND AFFILIATION

Decisions that don't make sense at first glance can often be explained by our relationship with status. As Godin writes, *"In human culture, status roles are everywhere that more than one human is present"* (Godin, loc. 1605). We are continuously seeking to either change or protect our status.

Key Takeaway: Status is relative.

Status is, by definition, about perception. It is defined by the person perceiving the status. There is no absolute value, and it can fluctuate depending on the person making the determination.

Key Takeaway: Status has inertia.

People are more likely to want to maintain their status than to try to change it. This is true of high status and low status alike.

Key Takeaway: Affiliation and domination are different measures of status.

You can spend your time helping others to increase their status, or you can hold others back in an attempt to boost your own status. Certain people/groups measure status through affiliation, while others value domination. However, modern society is primarily built around the concepts of affiliation and connection.

"Dominion is a vertical experience, above or below. Affiliation is a horizontal one: Who's standing next to me?" (Godin, loc. 1781). There is power in affiliation.

CHAPTER 12: A BETTER BUSINESS PLAN

This chapter outlines a new way of making a business plan. Godin divides his concept for a modern business plan into five sections: truth (specifics about the market you seek to enter), assertions (how you plan to make change), alternatives (what you will do when things don't go as planned), people (the attitudes and abilities of the people who will make up your team), and money (how much you need and how you will spend it).

Key Takeaway: The purpose of capitalism is to build culture, not vice versa.

Culture doesn't exist to serve capitalism. Marketers exist to engage with the culture, make change, and serve.

CHAPTER 13: SEMIOTICS, SYMBOLS, AND VERNACULAR

This chapter breaks down the concept of semiotics—the symbols we use to communicate—and the ways that marketers can invent new symbols. It all begins with the awareness that everyone perceives symbols differently.

Key Takeaway: People scan. They don't study.

When people see something new, they don't study it. They scan and make a quick assessment based on what it reminds them of. We rely on flags and symbols to signal whether we can trust something (or not).

Key Takeaway: A flag is a choice you need to make.

People will try to figure out who you are through scanning. The flags you present will serve as signals to them. Choosing not to present any flags to potential clients is not only lazy, but also foolish.

Key Takeaway: The value of your brand is determined by how much people care.

Your brand is a symbol of the promise you are making to the customer. You have to invest in your brand and make connections to get people to care. A logo means nothing without a brand behind it. Choose your logo carefully, but quickly, and stick with it. Invest your time in building your brand.

CHAPTER 14: TREAT DIFFERENT PEOPLE DIFFERENTLY

This chapter begins with a reminder that there are different groups of people that you need to serve. Only about fifteen percent of people are early adopters who love trying new things. Most people prefer to stick with what they already know. You will eventually reach those people horizontally, through other people, but first you have to start with your early adopters, who Godin calls "neophiliacs."

Key Takeaway: You can't teach someone who doesn't want to learn.

You can't teach someone against his or her will. You need to gain enrollment by asking for people's attention, not demanding it. Enrollment is mutual and consensual. You can't buy it. But once you have people's attention, given freely, you can begin to make real change.

Key Takeaway: Delight the few.

Because you have limited time and resources, you would be wise to invest them in extraordinary customers who are truly passionate about the change you're attempting to implement. You need to find those who are loyal to your product or service and treat them differently. Those people will then use their platforms to lead your cause to success.

CHAPTER 15: REACHING THE RIGHT PEOPLE

Godin outlines three important concepts presented in this chapter: goal, strategy, and tactics. Your goal is the change you want to make. Your tactics support your strategy. While your competition might try to steal your tactics, your strategy cannot be stolen. It is the way that you will attempt to accomplish your goal.

Key Takeaway: Online advertising is incredibly ignorant.

While online advertising has the benefit of being precise, instant, and highly measurable, it is also ignorant. This is due to the fact that people are automatically suspicious because they know that you're attempting to buy their attention. They are already inundated.

Key Takeaway: Measurement is the difference between direct and brand marketing.

"Direct marketing is action oriented. And it is measured. Brand marketing is culturally oriented. And it can't be measured" (Godin, loc. 2136).

You should measure everything when it comes to direct marketing because you need to know if your marketing is effective—that is, did it have the desired result? However, marketing your brand is not measurable. It is about engaging with the culture and being consistent. It requires time and patience.

Key Takeaway: Frequency is related to trust.

People remember things that they see many times. Creating memories requires repetition. Storytelling requires frequency. Frequency can be equated with trust.

CHAPTER 16: PRICE IS A STORY

In this chapter, Godin explores the idea of price as a signal. He explains that your price leads people to make certain assumptions about your product or service. Therefore, price can actually change what people think about your product or service.

Key Takeaway: Cheapest isn't necessarily best.

"When you're the cheapest, you're not promising change. You're promising the same, but cheaper" (Godin, loc. 2269).

Lowering your price can actually decrease consumers' trust in your product or service. This is often the case because spending money already sets people up to trust, due to cognitive dissonance. People don't want to think that they might be spending money on something worthless, so they will trust it.

Key Takeaway: Utilize the power of free.

Free ideas spread quickly, but you can't create tension or properly invest in your project when you have no cash flow. Therefore, you want to offer both free ideas and ideas that are worth paying for. A good example is music that is on the radio for free, but that the customer must pay for to hear in concert.

CHAPTER 17: PERMISSION AND REMARKABILITY IN A VIRTUOUS CYCLE

Being constantly inundated by advertisements trying to steal their time and money has made people jaded. The alternative is to engage on a personal level with anticipated and relevant communication.

Key Takeaway: Getting people's actual permission is extremely valuable.

Real permission is not legal permission. It's not given by ticking a required box on a form agreeing to a privacy policy. When people truly give you permission to engage with them, they will be concerned if you disappear. Permission marketing requires persistence and humility to earn and keep people's trust.

Key Takeaway: Make your project remarkable.

Your product or service should be one that people are eager to talk about. Godin calls this a "purple cow." This does not mean pulling stunts or going for shock value, which will lose you trust. Truly remarkable ideas will travel from person to person, horizontally.

CHAPTER 18: TRUST IS AS SCARCE AS ATTENTION

In this chapter, Godin explains how the internet is based on affiliation. This leads to a world in which being famous to only three thousand of the right people can be more than enough because those people will be able to spread the word. Fame and connection build trust and allow you to obtain the benefit of the doubt.

Key Takeaway: Trust is built through actions.

You earn trust through your actions. Too many marketers spend much too much time on words, when actions are where trust is developed. People will forget what you say, but they will remember what you did (or didn't do) for them. A trusted marketer follows through on his or her promises.

Key Takeaway: You need public relations more than publicity.

Public relations is about telling the right story in the right way to the right people—your smallest viable market.

CHAPTER 19: THE FUNNEL

In this chapter, Godin paints a picture of a funnel—a metaphor for the potential clients you lose along the way. You start with attention at the mouth of the funnel, but as it narrows, you lose people's attention and people "leak" out of the funnel. At the end, you are left with only a few loyal customers.

Key Takeaway: Work has a half-life.

By investing in a client before you get anything in return, you are investing in what Godin calls their "lifetime value." Over time, you will earn back what you have invested, and more! In fact, Godin considers that your first thousand customers are essentially priceless. In order to earn a profit, you need to know a customer's lifetime value. If your ad costs more than the lifetime value of the customers you have gained from running the ad, you will lose money.

Key Takeaway: Make "short heads" out of "long tails."

If you languish in the "long tail" of the market, it will be hard to make any profit. This is because the entire market has very, very few hits that achieve universal success, so most products fall somewhere in the long tail of mediocrity. The secret is to cut down the market in to many smaller curves. In doing so, you are better able to be the best at serving that particular niche market by making an extraordinary contribution that will place you in the short head (the "hits") of that market.

Key Takeaway: Remember the power of network effects.

Godin reminds readers of the power of connection and network effects, pointing out that ideas spread best in connected tribes. Early adopters are always trying new things, but most people only become aware of those ideas that are able to jump the chasm to being noticed.

Key Takeaway: In B2B marketing, give them the answers.

When you are marketing business-to-business (B2B), provide the buyer with the answer to the question he or she is asking him or herself: "How will I justify this purchase to the board/my boss/our investors?" The answer should match their narrative and the emotions their company values.

CHAPTER 20: ORGANIZING AND LEADING A TRIBE

This chapter focuses on Godin's concept of the tribe, defined as a group of people with shared goals, interests, and language. He emphasizes that you are there to organize and lead the tribe. The tribe does not belong to you. Your goal is simply for the tribe to listen to what you say. They don't need you, but would hopefully miss you if you went away.

Godin breaks down leading a tribe using Marshall Ganz's three-step action plan: "the story of self" (your platform), "the story of us" (the benefits of working together), and "the story of now" (getting the tribe engaged). As Godin says, if you are doing it right, your success should mean success for the tribe.

Key Takeaway: Behavior has a half-life.

Without maintenance, behavior will fade over time. You need to reinvest in your mission to avoid losing people to the next new thing.

CHAPTER 21: SOME CASE STUDIES USING THE METHOD

In this chapter, Godin explores some specific case studies of companies and organizations, such as Tesla and the NRA. He uses these examples to reinforce the ideas presented earlier in the book, including why creating tension and reaching the minimal viable audience are so successful.

CHAPTER 22: MARKETING WORKS, AND NOW IT'S YOUR TURN

This chapter is a brief collection of ideas that serve to inspire the reader while summing up the theories presented in earlier chapters.

Key Takeaway: Perfection is not the goal.

When you seek perfection, you set yourself up for failure. You should try to be better instead of trying to be perfect. If you can manage to be "good enough," you will be able to achieve the engagement that you need. In addition, you need to be able to seek help and give help because this creates connection, which can also help to achieve "better."

CHAPTER 23: MARKETING TO THE MOST IMPORTANT PERSON

This final chapter opens with a discussion of the moral value of marketing as Godin asks whether marketing can be considered to be "evil." He believes that the morality of marketing depends on the end goal: are you trying to help people or are your motives selfish and predatory? He again emphasizes the fact that marketing is about creating positive change and making things better.

Key Takeaway: Market to yourself first.

Godin reminds the reader that marketing is both a craft and a process. He believes that if you are finding it difficult to get started, you need to focus on marketing your idea to yourself first. The story you are telling yourself should fit your own narrative. You should be proud of what you are marketing.

EDITORIAL REVIEW

Seth Godin's book *This is Marketing: You Can't Be Seen Until You Learn to See,* challenges what you think you know about marketing, breaking it down into human elements and providing inspiration on how to create positive change. Godin insists that the path to better marketing is paved with empathy, and that you can only serve your clients once you understand them and their issues. Once you recognize that what they want is not the same as what you want, you will be empowered to help them solve important problems and ultimately make their lives better.

By turning traditional marketing logic on its head, Godin does away with the idea of starting with a product or service. He instead uses the metaphor of a lock and key to illustrate that the best marketing actually builds a key (product) for a lock (a client's problem), rather than making a key and searching high and low for a lock that the key will open. This logic feels sound, and while the reader may feel frustrated if he or she picked up the book hoping to find a magic solution to market an existing product or service, Godin's reasoning makes it clear that this attitude may be what is underlying the marketing problem to begin with.

As a confirmed expert in the marketing field, Godin draws much of the theory presented in this book from his previous work and that of other marketing experts, making it a one-stop-shop for key marketing concepts and innovative ideas. You can pick up this one book for a distilled version of modern marketing theory.

Godin backs up his theories with plenty of interesting case studies of the "big fish" in the marketplace, ranging from classic models of successful marketing, such as Apple, to highly unexpected examples of the power of the smallest viable market, such as the National Rifle Association.

While *This is Marketing* packs a punch, its thirty-two bite-sized chapters feel a bit fragmented at times, with the same concepts coming up at various points in different forms, with little structure linking between non-consecutive chapters, particularly towards the end of the book. This structure is, on one hand, highly digestible, but on the other, leaves the reader feeling like he or she is reading a collection of blog posts more than a single volume.

By highlighting the generosity of marketing done well, Godin's tone feels very positive and encouraging, almost like he's giving the reader a pep talk. His writing is accessible, and he leaves the reader feeling fully capable of making the world a better place. However, the book has a more philosophical than actionable tone, so it better suits a reader looking for inspiration and who can take Godin's idealistic theories with a pinch of salt.

All in all, *This is Marketing* is a fascinating read that will likely leave you wanting more. But with 18 other bestsellers to Godin's name, you are sure to find another read to expand upon the concepts presented in this book that resonated most with you.

BACKGROUND ON AUTHOR

Seth Godin is an American author, speaker, and entrepreneur with 19 best-selling books to his name. He has been inducted into the Direct Marketing Hall of Fame, the Guerrilla Marketing Hall of Fame, and the Marketing Hall of Fame.

For more than thirty years, Godin has aimed to teach, motivate, and inspire the masses to embrace the concept of marketing based on creating positive change.

His marketing blog is considered to be one of the most popular in the world, being named by *Time* magazine as one of the 25 best blogs of 2009. Godin has also given five TED talks, and he began producing a podcast called Akimbo in 2018.

Godin was born in Mount Vernon, New York in 1960. He earned a degree in computer science and philosophy from Tufts University in 1979. He then went on to receive his Masters in Business Administration from the Stanford Graduate School of Business in 1984, while simultaneously working his first job as a brand manager at Spinnaker Software, where he worked until 1986.

He then founded his own business, a book packaging company called Seth Godin Productions, using his savings. Godin subsequently founded another company called Yoyodyne, which he sold to Yahoo! for $30 million dollars in 1998. He then became Yahoo!'s vice president of permission marketing.

In 2000, Godin released a free e-book called *Unleashing the Ideavirus*, which is considered to be the most downloaded e-book in history. This served to further propel his prolific writing career, and set Godin on his way to becoming a household name.

Godin and his wife Helene have two sons. The family currently resides in New York.

OTHER TITLES BY SETH GODIN

The Smiley Dictionary. (1993).

eMarketing: Reaping Profits on the Information Highway. (1995).

Permission marketing: turning strangers into friends, and friends into customers. (1999).

If You're Clueless about Selling: And Want to Know More. (1998).

Unleashing the Ideavirus. (2001).

The Big Red Fez: How To Make Any Web Site Better. (2002).

Survival is not enough: zooming, evolution, and the future of your company. (2002).

Purple Cow: Transform Your Business by Being Remarkable. (2003).

Free Prize Inside!: The Next Big Marketing Idea. (2004).

All Marketers Are Liars: The Power of Telling Authentic Stories in a Low-Trust World. (2005).

The Big Moo: Stop Trying to be Perfect and Start Being Remarkable. (2005).

Small Is the New Big: and 193 Other Riffs, Rants, and Remarkable Business Ideas. (2006).

The Dip: A Little Book That Teaches You When to Quit (and When to Stick). (2007).

Meatball Sundae: Is Your Marketing out of Sync? (2008).

Tribes: We Need You to Lead Us. Portfolio. (2008).

Linchpin: Are You Indispensable? (2010).

Poke the Box. (2011).

We Are All Weird. The Domino Project. (2011).

The Icarus Deception: How High Will You Fly? (2012).

V Is for Vulnerable: Life Outside the Comfort Zone. (2012).

Whatcha Gonna Do with That Duck?: And Other Provocations. (2013).

What To Do When It's Your Turn (and it's always your turn) (2014).

END OF BOOK SUMMARY

If you enjoyed this ZIP Reads publication, we encourage you to purchase a copy of the original book.

We'd also love an honest review on Amazon.com!

Made in the USA
Monee, IL
28 October 2021